Angela Jain, Saira Alam, Hans-Liudger Dienel, Sabine Schröder,
Bhaskar Poldas, Julian Reimann

Participative Processes in the Field of Traffic and Transport

Emerging megacities
Dicussion Papers
Edited by Konrad Hagedorn, Christine Werthmann, Dimitrios Zikos, Ramesh Chennamaneni

Humboldt-Universität zu Berlin
Department of Agricultural Economics
Division of Resource Economics
Philippstr. 13, House 12
10115 Berlin

Tel.: +49 (0)30 2093 6305
Fax: +49 (0)30 2093 6497
www.agrar.hu-berlin.de/struktur/institute/wisola/fg/ress
www.sustainable-hyderabad.de

Contact: emerging.megacities@hu-berlin.de

The emerging megacities discussion papers are available at:
www.eh-verlag.de

ISSN print edition 2193-6927

Emerging megacities Discussion Papers are prepared by researchers working on topics in the realm of sustainable development in Megacities of Tomorrow, a research priority by the German Ministry of Education and Research (BMBF). The papers have been peer-reviewed by a board of external reviewers.
Views and opinions expressed do not necessarily represent those of the Division of Resource Economics.
Comments are highly welcome and should be sent directly to the authors.
We welcome contributions on any topics related to Megacities of Tomorrow. Further information on the submission procedure is given at:
www.sustainable-hyderabad.de/emerging-megacities

Jain, Angela; Alam, Saira; Dienel, Hans-Liudger; Schröder, Sabine; Poldas, Bhaskar; Reimann, Julian

Participative Processes in the Field of Traffic and Transport

Emerging megacities Discussion Papers, Volume 7/2010

ISBN/EAN: 978-3-86741-824-9

First published in 2012 by Europaeischer Hochschulverlag GmbH & Co KG, Bremen, Germany.

© Europaeischer Hochschulverlag GmbH & Co KG, Fahrenheitstr. 1, D-28359 Bremen (www.eh-verlag.de). All rights reserved.

Cover: Photo "Metropolis", ferendus (flickr). Creative Commons License

No part of this publication may be reproduced or transmitted, in any form or by any means, electronic, mechanical, photocopying, recording or otherwise, or stored in any retrieval system of nay nature, without the written permission of the copyright holder and the publisher, application for which shall be made to the publisher.

EHV

Participative Processes in the Field of Traffic and Transport

Angela Jain[*][†], *Saira Alam*[†], *Hans-Liudger Dienel*[†], *Sabine Schröder*[†], *Bhaskar Poldas*[†], *Julian Reimann*[†]

September 2010

Abstract

Due to a constantly high population growth of India's sixth largest metropolis Hyderabad, a strongly growing middle-class and the subsequent rise of traffic and motorised vehicles in particular, sustainable solutions are needed to secure daily routines. For up to 50 % of the – predominantly poor – population, walking is crucial for everyday life. There is a tendency towards suburbanisation, still, for many people living in the city's central areas even low fares for busses or rickshaws are often not affordable. Additionally, the high level of air pollution poses a risk for people's health.

This paper presents the action research conducted in 2009 (Citizens' Exhibition, expert workshop and online-dialogue). It analyses the degree of participation at different levels and evaluates the participative tools and methods used. It explains the most important problems in the field of traffic and transport from the citizens' point of view on the local level and gives an outlook on the problems and tasks at the city level.

The analysis shows that the situation of pedestrians can be seen as one of the most important problems in the field of traffic and transport: a high rate of fatal accidents in which pedestrians lose their lives. Also missing or unattractive footpaths lead to a high probability of switching over to motorised transport modes by those pedestrians who can afford it and to the marginalisation of those who cannot afford it. At the same time the topic bears good opportunities to come up with low-tech, cost effective and at the same time highly efficient solutions in terms of CO_2 reduction. Although or for the reason that the topic is not on the top list of the political agenda, there is a civil movement to push it forward and forcefully improve mobility and quality of life.

Key words: *participation, participative process, citizens' exhibition, citizens' charter, traffic, transport, Hyderabad, India*

---

[*] Corresponding author. Tel.: +49 30 3180 5466. Email: jain@nexusinstitut.de
[†] nexus - Institute for Cooperation Management and Interdisciplinary Research GmbH, Otto-Suhr-Allee 59, Berlin

1 Introduction

As Hyderabad is a rapidly emerging Megacity with already approximately seven million inhabitants, many complex traffic and transportation problems exist in the metropolitan area and different mass transportation systems are being discussed. The vehicular traffic is one major factor which greatly influences the greenhouse gas emissions in Hyderabad. In 2008, there were a total of 2.4 Million vehicles in Hyderabad. Due to a constant rise in the number of vehicles at an estimated rate of 0.2 million per annum, the total vehicle population is projected to reach 7.4 million by 2025[1]. Nevertheless, a high percentage of travel in Indian megacities is by walking or cycling, mainly because many inhabitants are too poor to afford motorised or even public transport. But decentralisation has affected urban transport: the expansion of the cities has increased the length of trips for most urban residents leading to more overall travel demand and thus more traffic on the roadways and public transport systems. Moreover, increased trip distances make walking and cycling less feasible than before. Currently, the construction of a Metro Rail system for Hyderabad is discussed very controversially among experts, politicians and civil society. In the spring of 2009, due to financial constraints, the project has temporarily been put on hold, in 2010 the negotiations have started again with the result that the Hyderabad metro will be built from 2011 on. At the same time phase II of the MMTS-Railway system is going to be realised. Non-motorised transport modes have not been integrated into the transport system so far, but it is high time to promote them now.

A main focus within the project is to develop a sustainable, energy efficient and also inclusive transportation management scheme by integrating citizens' views and needs into the planning process at local level. Sustainable transportation planning aims at providing a safe, climate friendly, cost-effective and equitable transportation system.

As reports show (cf. Kern et al. 2009), there is basically no knowledge about the demand side of the traffic system; citizens have not been asked which kind of transport they prefer. Does the traffic and transportation system meet the needs of Hyderabad's citizens? How can it be organised in a way that it is safer, more secure, and citizen-friendly and energy efficient at the same time?

Based on the Background Study "Constraints and Opportunities for Participation and Communication" (Nexus Institute 2009), nexus observes current planning processes at

---

[1] Engineers Staff College of India (ESCI): Presentation by Dr. S. Nagabhushana Rao on a Scenario Workshop within the Sustainable Hyderabad Project. Hyderabad, March 2009.

the city level (master plan and transport study), and exchanges its views and ideas about citizens' participation with planners and officials (e.g. from ADAPT and HMDA). This aims to increase the options for citizens to raise their voice and to improve institutions and governance structures to systematically include the perspectives of citizens into city development.

Information, communication and participation are very essential processes for any project, which aims at the implementation of integrated planning and the development of improved governance structures. Participative and communicative approaches are essential to create and increase awareness for the consequences of climate change, mitigation- and adaptation strategies among affected stakeholders. It is likewise crucial to integrate the local knowledge and the needs of the affected groups in developing strategies and to activate the stakeholders to take self-initiative. The discussion on the reasons and consequences of climate change is taking place at different levels today, but is only marginally reaching the population. To ensure a sustainable growth process, co-operation between stakeholders of civil society, economy and science in developing political strategies is needed. This should include intensive discussions on the reasons and consequences of climate change, which not only focus on possibilities to solve the problems politically, but also includes possibilities of self-action in daily routines. Thus, communication and participation strategies have a major influence on the CO_2 and other greenhouse gas emissions. This is especially the case when it comes to the citizens' choice of transport modes or the building of new traffic infrastructure without integrating the people's demands within the decision processes. Therefore, the project partners developed and implemented innovative and activating tools for participation and communication to foster communication, co-operation and participation in Hyderabad. In this context nexus also works on the development and implementation of pilot projects, in cooperation with other WPs of the project and Indian partners as well as in tune with the actor's analysis.

All of the envisaged pilot projects are planned and will be implemented in a way that they meet the following demands:

- strengthen participation of citizens and civil society groups;
- foster energy efficiency and CO_2 reduction;
- include capacity building / awareness raising measures;
- integrate the three dimensions of sustainability.

To promote networking for analysis and action, the participative processes have been jointly organised with partners in close collaboration with civil society organisations in Hyderabad. During the discussion the problems associated to the traffic situation and transport system in Hyderabad recurred many times as a problem that affects almost every citizen in different ways. In this context also the responsible authorities for planning, construction and maintenance of traffic infrastructure were identified (Chapter 2). Thereby, a comprehensive stakeholder analysis is greatly necessary to initiate a sustainable stakeholder dialogue that includes all involved groups – citizens and administration.

The methodological approaches and the specific measures undertaken by the project partners are explained (Chapter 3). Former studies (cf. Poldas 2011, PIK 2010) showed that the inhabitants of Hyderabad indeed are highly affected by traffic and infrastructural problems, but the awareness of the context between personal behaviour and climate change plus related aspects is rather low. In order to answer the former named questions and to bring the topic of traffic and transportation to the fore, a Citizens' Exhibition "Ready to Move...?!" was organised by the project and shown in Tarnaka Ward and at the occasion of several conferences and summits in Hyderabad. At the same time, an online discussion forum voicing questions similar to the ones in the course of the exhibition was launched, trying to gather the broad public's opinion on these urgent topics, their vision and solutions. Subsequently, a conference on traffic and transport was organised by nexus in collaboration with PTV, Goethe Centre Hyderabad and Right to Walk Foundation. It was aimed at formulating a "Hyderabad Citizens' Charter for Urban Transport".

2 Stakeholder Analysis

The analysis in preparation of the participative processes showed that there is a civil movement which aims at the improvement of the traffic situation and the transport system and hence the quality of life. There is also rising awareness on the political and planners level. The deficit becomes apparent – as often – at the implementation level.

It can be assumed that the cause is related to 'large-scale thinking' on the one hand and unclear responsibilities on the other hand. It therefore seems to be meaningful to focus on the local level (small scale) in the first step and work out functional solutions in a bottom-up process with the help of local knowledge. In the second step these solutions can be transformed and up scaled to city level.

The Background Study "Constraints and Opportunities for Participation and Communication" already listed organisations active in the field of traffic and transport. The relevant organisations identified have become cooperation partners of the project. Their initiatives and campaigns are summed up below. Additionally the function and interaction of involved authorities on the state and local level is described.

It is interesting to note that the argumentation for a better public transport does not primarily originate from an environmental argumentation, but rather from a social and aesthetic point of view, i.e. public transport has to be made accessible to all and it has to be more comfortable and faster. Furthermore the relationship between authorities among themselves as well as between authorities and citizens appears strained. While there is a formal responsibility for roads and sidewalks in Hyderabad, the operational responsibility is unsolved. Lacking any kind of participative procedures within the official decision-making processes several civil society organisations established in recent times. They bundle the citizens' interests and emphasise their demands especially regarding to large-scale infrastructure projects like the Metro or omnipresent problems such as missing and encroached footpaths.

2.1 Civil Society Organisations

2.1.1 Citizens for Better Public Transport in Hyderabad (CBPTH)

CBPTH is a coalition of about 50 civil society organisations and individuals who would like to generate a public debate and involve the civil society on the options for public transportation in Hyderabad. CBPTH believes that a metropolitan transport authority with representatives from the concerned departments, peoples' representatives and civil society should be constituted. CBPTH demands improvement in public transport infrastructure, pedestrian pathways along the roads and zebra crossings at all intersections and bus stops. There should be no road without a footpath.

- In a Citizen Declaration for Better Public Transport in Hyderabad (2007), CBPTH demanded that a number of measures are to be implemented as a package with a strong political will to reduce congestion, "save people's time and money", improve air quality, and promote public health by making public transportation a comfortable and dignified experience for citizens in Hyderabad.

- CBPTH is one of the few voices which have consistently questioned the government's decision on building an elevated metro rail track in Hyderabad rather than putting efforts in the improvement of the existing MMTS (Multi Modal Transit System) by taking up phase II of MMTS (Exhibition in 2008).

2.1.2 Right to Walk Foundation (R2W)

Ms. Kanthimathi Kannan started the Right to Walk Foundation in 2005 to make Hyderabad a pedestrian friendly city. The mission of R2W is to educate the Government and the citizens of Hyderabad about the importance of footpaths. To achieve these goals, Ms. Kannan has been submitting applications and filing petitions under the Right to Information Act (RTI Act), to urge the city government to make the roads pedestrian-friendly with proper footpaths and to clear responsibilities and integrate footpaths into city and transport planning.

- "20k Signature Campaign" 2008. Signatures of those who are most affected due to lack of footpaths like children, women, senior citizens and disabled were collected.

- A Walkathon was conducted on Feb 17, 2009. The Goethe-Centre and the R2W coordinated with Vidyaranya School and conducted a "Study Walk".

- R2W also aims at conducting Walkability Studies. This fairly scientific method gives a few guidelines to enable the walker to decide how walkable a stretch is. The R2W is involving students from the urban planning department of JNAFAU, Masab Tank in the study.

2.1.3 Association of German Culture Hyderabad (AGCH) – Goethe Zentrum Hyderabad

The Goethe-Centre Hyderabad has the same primary aim as the Goethe-Institutes all over the world (in India called Max-Müller-Bhavans, MMB). The primary aim of Goethe-Centre is to promote knowledge of the German language, German culture and foster inter-cultural cooperation. Besides constantly organising various cultural events with Indian, German and international artists, it is engaged in many social and developmental activities. Through its many contacts in Hyderabad's civil society, public authorities, experts and economy the Goethe-Centre can play an important role as a multiplicator.

- In 2008, the Goethe-Centre organised an exhibition on the impacts of the planned Metro Rail project on Hyderabad city in close co-operation with CSOs like Right to Walk Foundation, Forum for a Better Hyderabad, Citizens for Better Public Transport Hyderabad (CBPTH) etc.

- It organises social events by involving school children and citizens of Hyderabad. On 17th February 2009, in co-operation with Right to Walk Foundation, it organised a Study-Walk with the students of Vidyaranya School to raise their awareness about the traffic situation and their rights in traffic.

2.1.4 The Indian Youth Climate Network (IYCN) / Hyderabad Climate Alliance

IYCN works to generate awareness about and establish consensus on what role India should play in the global debate of climate change, and how it should address its domestic issues. Within its short term of existence, the network has seen massive growth and has generated a lot of awareness in India and internationally. The Hyderabad Climate Alliance is a wing of the Indian Youth Climate Network (IYCN). It was established in 2008 in the context of the Indian Youth Summit on Climate Change organised by the Indian Youth Climate Network and its partners.

- In 2008 Hyderabad celebrated a momentous occasion, as the nation's first Youth Summit on Climate Change took place, organised by the IYCN. The IYCN in Hyderabad organised the Hyderabad Youth Summit on Climate Change on June $21^{st}/22^{nd}$ 2009.
- Every month the Hyderabad Climate Alliance organises a bicycle rallye through the city to raise awareness about climate change. Above this, no other activities related to traffic and transport have been organised so far, but are intended.

2.1.5 Tarnaka Residents' Welfare Association (TRWA)

The Tarnaka Residents Welfare Associations is a nationally as well as internationally notable community concept which is – disappointed due to a lack of political mediation through representation at the level of urban governance – trying to find new forms of self-management and development within its small range of community level. The Residents Welfare Association builds the core of social consensus and is also well aware of all the diversity that exists in the local community. An informal but well-structured Ward Sabha, comparable to the Gram Sabha at village level, is regularly held and represents the TRWAs expression of direct democracy. The Ward Sabha adopts a micro-plan for the area's development. Within these considerations, local level executive officials of different departments are invited to participate and enrich the debates by technical insight information.

2.2 State Authorities

2.2.1 Department for Transport Roads and Buildings

The Transport Roads & Buildings department of Andhra Pradesh deals with the construction, maintenance and administrative aspects of traffic and transport. The department also deals with the construction of certain public buildings that belong to the Government of Andhra Pradesh.[2] The department is acting as umbrella organisation for different department wings which have different impacts in the field of traffic and transportation in Hyderabad.

Thereby, the Transport Department is responsible for administrative measures, driving licenses, vehicle registrations, special permits as well as fees and taxes. Thus, this wing has a mediate influence on local traffic while possessing opportunities to regulate the type and quantity of vehicles and drivers. Further functions of the department are to "assist other organisations in the development of transport facilities in the state [and to] develop an efficient transport system [...] that enables the transfer of passengers and goods in a cost efficient manner"[3] In comparison to that the Roads & Buildings department wing is responsible for planning, building and maintenance of national highways, causeways, bridges and connecting roads in the state of Andhra Pradesh. This jurisdiction also applies on the local level within the city of Hyderabad and this constellation is predestined to lead to functional and administrative overlaps with local authorities.

The Andhra Pradesh State Road Transport Corporation (APSRTC) serves as provider for the public bus transport in the state. This includes long-distance traffic in rural areas, connections between the cities and local public transport, e.g. in Hyderabad. It is easily to imagine that covering these different tasks and areas in combination with a fast growing and more mobile population is hard to fulfil.

2.2.2 Department for Municipal Administration and Urban Development

"The Department of Municipal Administration and Urban Development handles planning and development in urban and rural areas. The development is achieved through Master Plans prepared for urban centres and rural areas."[4] It assists in town and country planning matters and is especially responsible for the coordination with other departments involved in development schemes. With regard to the area of Hyderabad

---

[2] APOnline: List of Organisations by Department: Transport Roads and Buildings. www.aponline.gov.in/apportal/departments/portallistoforgsbydepts.aspx?i=3 [29-12-11].
[3] Ibid.
[4] Ibid.

the department is the supreme authority for two important actors in the field of traffic: HMDA and GHMC.

2.3 Local Authorities

2.3.1 Hyderabad Metropolitan Development Authority (HMDA)

HMDA's range of authority includes the city of Hyderabad and surrounding municipalities. Thus, it covers an area of 7,100 km^2 and is the second largest urban development area in India after Bangalore. It was set up for the purposes of planning, co-ordination, supervising, promoting and securing the planned development of the Hyderabad Metropolitan Region. Additionally it coordinates the development activities of the municipal corporations, municipalities and other local authorities.[5] Furthermore, HMDA is directly responsible for the planning and construction of main roads and flyovers within the metropolitan area.

2.3.2 Greater Hyderabad Municipal Corporation (GHMC)

GHMC is Hyderabad's municipal administration since 2007. It is responsible for basic needs and nearly all facets of urban life including property taxes, trade licenses and town planning. The mayor of Hyderabad is the titular head of GHMC, but the executive power is in the hands of the Municipal Commissioner who is delegated by the government of Andhra Pradesh. Regarding the issue of transportation GHMC is responsible for the construction maintenance of roads and especially sidewalks.

2.3.3 Hyderabad Traffic Police

The traffic police must be named as a stakeholder because of its intermediate position. While confronted with the often chaotic traffic situation the traffic police is the first contact for the population. In addition, it is the police that is collecting accident and traffic behaviour data for statistic purposes. When thinking about specific improvement measures the involvement of the traffic police is indispensible because of its function as authority with first-hand information and its main task: the enforcement of (new) legal regulations.

---

[5] HMDA: About us. www.hmda.gov.in/ [30-12-11]

2.3.4 An Intermediate Joint Committee: Unified Metropolitan Transport Authority (UMTA)

Since 2008 the UMTA is one of the HMDA committees with a special composition of the members. Among others they belong to local and state authorities, police, APSRTC and South Central Railway. It should enhance and ensure effective coordination of traffic and transportation measures undertaken by different agencies. This includes the field of public transport systems as well as questions of projects' funding or monitoring major traffic and transportation projects. The UMTA sub-committee is to monitor and effectively implement the decisions of UMTA.

The UMTA could become an effective tool for comprehensive, sustainable urban planning. The establishment process took almost 20 years; its abilities should be proved soon.

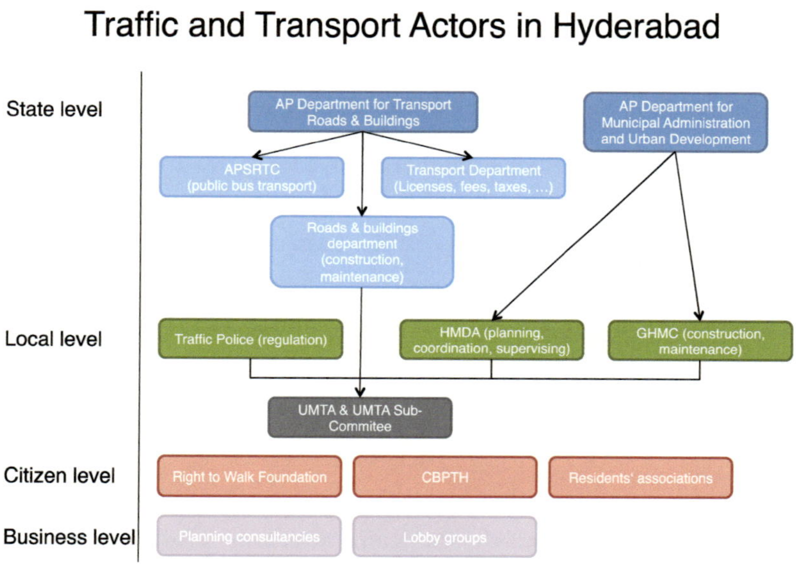

Figure 1: Traffic and Transport Actors in Hyderabad

3 Participatory Processes

Today participation – codetermination, involvement, contribution – is an important factor in public and societal work. Participation means involvement of all the relevant persons and groups in processes of cooperation that call for joint decision-making.

Successful cooperation requires participation. Participation creates motivation, commitment, responsibility and trust, making it relevant for groups, teams, departments, projects and organisations. Participative methods are flexible and can be applied in various contexts and problem fields and to groups of different sizes. They support procedures for developing, planning and carrying out change processes in companies, administrations, education, research and citizenry. Furthermore, they ensure that the great number of persons contribute to the process, make use of existing creativity, experiences and the participants' potential in various ways and allow for a variety of ideas for solutions.

Important in the Indian context is the fact that participation also raises the level of acceptance and viability of decisions. The emphasis here is on developing ideas together, gaining knowledge as a group and acting jointly. Until now, this approach is rather uncommon in India and Hyderabad in particular. In the field of traffic and transportation participation gives a voice to those affected – the citizens – and encourages people to take self-initiative instead of obstinately accepting top-down decisions.

3.1 Legal Bases: Right to Information & Public Interest Litigation

Generally, participatory processes are quite difficult to implement, not only in the Indian context but also in other countries – even though it should be part of any democracy. In many developing countries, modernisation and colonialism undermined indigenous social relations. After World War II, governments increasingly assumed a wider range of responsibility in governing nation states. "However, the growing disenchantment of ordinary people with the institutions of the state has resulted in the resurgence of civil society." (Mohanty 2005)

In India a wide variety of civil society activity can be seen, yet such activity appears not to lead to empowerment for those who need it the most. "For the least empowered, a lack of education, wealth, land, and other factors continues to hinder the access to power through civil society structures." (Mohanty 2005)

The Indian Civil Society Movement is quite weak compared to 36 other countries worldwide, but slightly above average in comparison to developing and transitional countries. Of the economically active population in India only 1.4 % is active in a Civil Society Organisation, most of them as volunteers.

Thus, while at first glance, civil society activity has grown in recent decades in India, such mass participation in itself is not proof of mass empowerment. India has a perfectly legitimate, democratically elected government, but its governance of the country's economic and social resources leaves much to be desired. (Mohanty 2005) The voice of

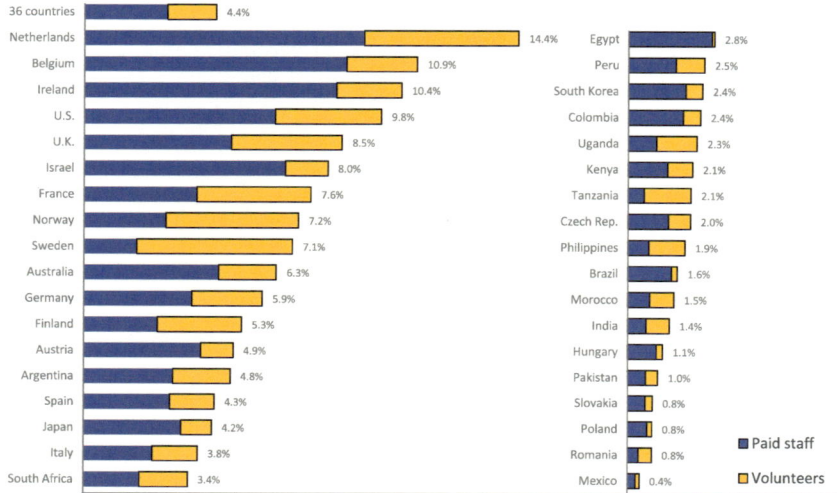

Figure 2: Civil society organisation workforce as a share of the economically active population
Source: Center for Civil Society Studies: Comparative Data
http://ccss.jhu.edu/publications-findings?did=308 [14-07-10]

civil society is not strong enough to push forward formalised or even informal participative processes. Moreover, participatory activities are hardly able to overcome barriers of status and caste in India. The Citizens' Charter Conference, for example, mainly had participants from people of the urban middle class. Nonetheless the Citizens' Exhibition did cover all different kinds of people.

A reason for the weak engagement assumingly is the disappointment and distrust regarding the accountability of governance structures and politicians. "There is constant suspicion that potential allies might, in truth, be pursuing a hidden, illegitimate agenda, that one might deprive another of well-earned claims to fame, or that they might only be attempting to siphon off foreign funds. This lack of trust reflects a malfunctioning administrative structure. Generally speaking, government appears to be unreliable and unaccountable. It does not adequately implement its own legislation." (Dembowski 2001)

But as experienced in the course of the project, many people are willing to take part in decision making. It is no problem for citizens to state and discuss their opinions. However, in most cases Civil Society can only react to situations or occurrences in retrospect. Poor enforcement of regulations makes citizens to act in ways other than alerting public enforcement agencies. Frequently the case is won by individuals using two legal instruments: Right to Information Act (RTI) and Public Litigation Interest (PIL) (Santhakumar 2009, Nexus Institute 2009).

It has become clear that India's 1.2 billion citizens have been empowered by the far-reaching law granting them the right to demand almost any information from the government. India's Right to Information law has given a powerful tool to civil society, especially the poor who have no political lobby. The law, passed after more than a decade of agitation by good-government activists, has become embedded in Indian folklore. It finally took the intervention by the Supreme Court through a PIL filed by the NCPRI (National Campaign on People's Right to Information) until the Right to Information Act was finally enacted in October 2005, taking into account recommendations of civil society groups.

In the first three years the law was in effect, two million applications were filed. The law is backed by stiff fines for bureaucrats who withhold information, a penalty that appears to be ensuring speedy compliance. "But a more responsive bureaucracy is not necessarily less corrupt." (Kumar & Sokol 2010) Some critics wonder if the law is simply a pressure valve that allows people to get basic needs addressed without challenging the status quo. "It has been very successful in rooting out petty corruption," said Venkatesh Nayak of the Commonwealth Human Rights Initiative. "Our accountability mechanisms are weak, and transparency has no purpose without accountability." But still the law has had its effect as the main objective was to empower citizens. "This law has done that — given the people the power to challenge their government. That is no small thing."

Public Interest Litigation (PIL) is a progressive – and in most other countries uncommon – feature of the Indian system which allows organisations or individuals to take legal action on behalf of a third party. It is most often used in cases where persons directly affected by an illegal action are unable (financially, emotionally, physically, due to illiteracy) to fight the case themselves. PIL is thus an important forum for civil society to stake their claims. It has been on the rise since the 1980s and CSOs (Civil Society Organisations) have increasingly used the tool to stake their claims. While most of the cases dealt with social issues until the 1980s, their contents changed to environmental issues and those of administrative behaviour in the 1990s.

The Supreme Court recently announced the creation of second "special green bench" to deal with matters relating to environment and forest in view of manifold increase in number of such cases (ZEENEWS 2010). This can be attributed to the fact that PIL is increasingly initiated by elites, making this progressive legal instrument more and more dominated by the middle and upper class.

Through PIL courts have been forced to assume the role of activators and regulators. The Courts examine complaints filed under the environmental laws either by the regulators at the magistrate level or by citizens and civil society groups directly with the higher courts which exercise original jurisdiction under Public Interest Litigation. And some groundbreaking decisions have been made by the courts in the sector of consumer and environmental protection (Chatterjee 2009). In fact, the PILs filed directly in courts by a pollution victim or community have been more effective than prosecution under the Indian Environmental Act on the impact-area focus (Jariwala 2004). But in the end these have been one time directions for clean up or remediation without any programmatic follow up. Moreover, the impact of PIL is limited due to the lack of power of enforcement of the courts and an inherently slow judicial administration.

3.2 The Citizens' Exhibition

3.2.1 Method

The Citizens' Exhibition and the previous survey visualise personal perspectives on the process of finding solutions and present them to a large group of people. The exhibition is designed to provide information, inspire further discussion and add transparency to a process of discussion or change. It represents a relatively new method of public participation, presenting the local people's views and attitudes in the form of excerpts from interviews together with photographs of the people and their urban quarter in a public exhibition, and thus linking participative elements with aesthetic components, affording a visual impression and experience of various persons, players and group representatives and their personal perspectives, attitudes and desires. The objective of the Citizens' Exhibition is to present the goals and motivation of stakeholders – such as the residents in a neighbourhood, the municipal administration, private investors – and thus to spur public dialogue and promote understanding concerning the selected issue. In addition, plans and activities can be made transparent. The joint exhibition can contribute to a stronger identification of the participants with their group, with the goals of their activities, and with their neighbourhood, while at the same time increasing the understanding for the viewpoints of other interest groups. The major strength of the approach is the aesthetic and emotional power of pictures in combination with the relevant quotations

(Dienel, Schophaus 2002). The points of view in the public can be examined in a direct way, and statements can be linked to specific individuals and places.

In Hyderabad a Citizens' Exhibition regarding the issue of traffic and transportation was organised (Böhm et al. (not yet published)) in co-operation with the "Tarnaka Residents Welfare Association". The topic for the Citizens' Exhibition was chosen in cooperation with the Tarnaka Residents' Welfare association. The method of the Citizens' Exhibition is comprised of the following stages:

At first, it is necessary to select an appropriate topic that should ideally be a matter that every citizen can refer to. If possible the topic should be selected in cooperation with representatives from the involved interest groups (Böhm et al. 2008). In the case of the Tarnaka Citizens' Exhibition the topic was selected in cooperation with the Tarnaka Residents Welfare Association.

In a second step, the interview partners were identified. It is important to clarify whether a group wants to present themselves and the topic they are concerned about, or whether the focus should be placed on cooperation and conflicts between various stakeholders, all of which should then be interviewed (e.g. local residents, administration, businesses). It is advisable to select interview partners with differing profiles (on the principle of contrasts), in order to provide the broadest possible range of views about a problem. This also means that numerically underrepresented perspectives will find a voice in the discussion. In a third step, the semi-structured qualitative interviews were conducted. For the Citizens' Exhibition "Ready to Move...?!" we did not identify specific interview partners beforehand, but interviewed inhabitants of Tarnaka or those who regularly come to Tarnaka. In total 24 respondents answered the survey, either on the street or at their home or bureau spontaneously, as traffic and transportation is a topic that every citizen can refer to[6]. We looked for a broad range of views and thus interviewed citizens varying in sex, age, background and occupation (school children, elderly, businessmen, rickshaw drivers, street food vendors, housewives and representatives of the local administration) in Tarnaka to find out which problems different citizens face in transportation and traffic every day and what kind of solutions they suggest for a sustainable traffic and transportation. The interviews are recorded and transcribed literally. The qualitative interviews are designed in such a way that the interviewees are able to talk extensively about their personal view and perspective of the topic. During or after the interview a picture of the interviewees is taken for the poster of the exhibition. Further pictures were taken of different situations in traffic that the interviewees talked

---

[6] In the Indian context the spontaneous interviewing did not pose a problem to most people.

about to visualise their views. Another option would be to ask the interviewees to take these pictures themselves.

In the next step the images and excerpts of the interviews are prepared for a public exhibition. This exhibition can be prepared on a very low budget, but the exhibits should always combine images and texts so that the inner views can be presented in more detail. The texts should be short, characteristic excerpts from the interviews. For the exhibition 14 posters including pictures and interviews were produced in English and Telugu in each case.

Finally, the opening of the exhibition plays a key role. (Dienel, Schophaus 2002) All the participating interest groups can be invited to come together, along with interested members of the public. For the opening it is important that the venue is a local one. The participants are highly motivated to come to this opening event, because they will find themselves in the exhibition. In addition to its public impact, another very important aspect of the exhibition opening is the opportunity it provides for initiating dialogue within and between the interest groups. This can take place either informally while looking at the exhibition or in a structured form by integrating further participation processes in the exhibition.

3.2.2 Realisation

In the case of Tarnaka, the Citizens' Exhibition was inaugurated on March 1st, 2009 within the "5th Ward Sabha" (Ward meeting) of the Tarnaka Residents' Welfare Association in the community hall of Tarnaka. A large number of residents from Tarnaka and Hyderabad and representatives from Osmania University, Hyderabad, and from Delhi and Bangalore were present. The exhibition was on display until the middle of March 2009 in the community hall of Tarnaka. In June 2009 it was shown on the Hyderabad Youth Summit on Climate Change. On both events reactions of visitors were captured on paper to collect more views from the visitors. It is planned to show the Citizens' Exhibition "Ready to Move...?!" in further public buildings in Hyderabad. The attention generated through the citizens' exhibition for the matter of sustainable traffic shall be utilised to develop new projects to reduce emissions in traffic and to raise awareness for the topic of an energy-efficient transport and traffic system.

The interviews with Tarnaka residents showed that all of the interviewees were very aware of and to a more or lesser extent affected by the different problems associated with the traffic and transportation situation in Hyderabad. However, the interviews also showed that the traffic problem is primarily perceived as a safety (e.g. low safety

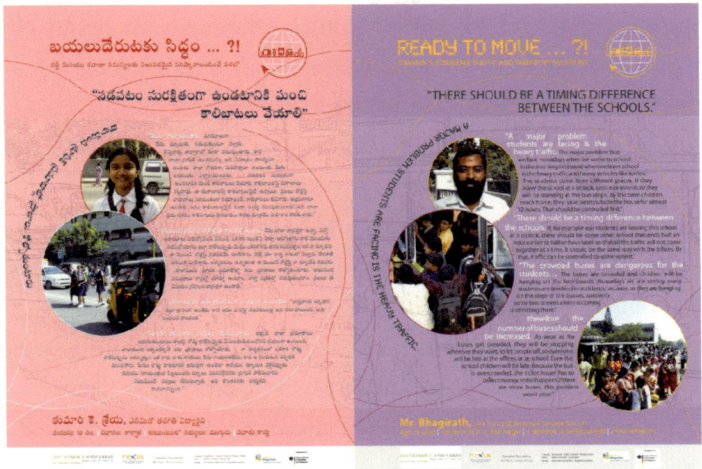

Figure 3: Poster of the Citizens' Exhibition in Telugu and in English

for pedestrians, too many accidents) and time problem (traffic jams and long commuting times) rather than as an environmental problem. Although the awareness of Indian people for the issue of climate change is rising according to recent polls, people seem not to connect the issue to everyday life situations or problems. Interestingly, strong pollution was not named in the interviews as one of the major problems of the heavy traffic, but rather the long commuting times, an inadequate public transportation system, the disobeying of traffic rules and the lack of safety in traffic especially for pedestrians. This shows that awareness raising and activation of citizens for climate related problems have to use these aspects as starting points. These must then be linked to the issue of climate change and the necessity of energy efficiency and mitigation.

The problems mentioned by the interviewees can be categorised into two main issues: 1. lack of safety and 2. an inadequate public transportation system. (Both are caused by heavy traffic and are on the other hand leading to more traffic.)

The lack of safety especially for pedestrians was seen as a severe problem by many interviewees leading to a high number of traffic accidents involving especially pedestrians and motorcycles. This lack of safety is mainly caused by missing or obstructed footpaths, a lack of pedestrian crossings and traffic signals on big streets and the disobeying of traffic rules by motorists. At many places in Hyderabad there is no infrastructure for pedestrians to cross the street. Although there are traffic lights at major junctions, crossing the street at a signal can still pose a problem, as traffic rules and signals are often not obeyed. Lately, traffic police is more or less successfully trying to regulate some junctions in Hyderabad to ensure traffic discipline. In many places there are no signals, zebra crossings or foot over bridges at all and crossing the street basically means working your way across lane by lane, waiting for a small spot between two cars. Especially for children and elderly people this poses a great problem that limits their mobility: *"Crossing the road is very, very difficult. Many times I will be taking assistance of young fellows. [...] They should have zebra crossing and on both sides of traffic they should stop with signals. When there is a red light the traffic should not flow. Then they should allow us to cross"* (Interviewee, 73 years old). Another issue leading to a lack of safety for pedestrians, which is often mentioned and discussed in Hyderabad are the missing or obstructed footpaths. In Hyderabad, the footpaths – if existing at all– are mostly obstructed by parking cars or motorcycles, by street vendors, businesses or home owners, which forces pedestrians to use the crowded streets as walkways: *"The footpaths are all occupied by fruit vendors, hawkers and small businesses. Wherever you stand there is a guy selling fruit"* (Interviewee, 38 years).

Some of the solutions suggested to improve safety were to build more zebra crossings and signals. In order to arrive at more traffic discipline, children should already be taught in school about traffic behaviour: *"Regarding discipline and traffic sense, we don't educate the children in schools. So, I think we should start from the childhood, educating the children how to discipline yourself while you are moving."* Furthermore, in order to clear the footpaths and make them usable for pedestrians, cars and auto rickshaws should be provided more parking spaces and food vendors should be provided appropriate vending spaces without dislocating them from their established customers.

Another major issue mentioned in the interviews is the inadequate public transport system, which causes more people to choose the car or motorcycle over public transport facilities. In Hyderabad, there is a train system (Multi-Modal Transport System, MMTS) with two lines, going around one half of the inner city without entering the inner city. Other public transport means are the buses – city lines as well as regional buses. The auto rickshaws can also be seen as a supplementary means of public transport similar to taxis. During peak hours, the buses in Hyderabad are heavily overcrowded and follow no specified time schedule. It is hardly possible for children, women and elderly people to enter a bus that arrives already overcrowded. This on the one hand leads to very long waiting hours for school children and students before and after school and on the other hand makes going by bus unattractive. *"The students come from different places. If they leave the school at 5 o'clock, until 6 or 6:30 they will be standing in the bus stop. By the time children reach home they have been outside the house for almost 12 hours"* an interviewed teacher stated.

According to the interviewed persons these obstacles could be reduced by strengthening and extending the existing MMTS. Furthermore, the connectivity between the MMTS and buses as well as between buses should be improved. Furthermore, to reduce traffic, crowded buses and waiting hours at peak times and thus make buses more attractive, the number of buses should be increased as well as the timings of schools, offices and shops should be differentiated, so that there is less traffic during peak hours and buses can be more reliable. This concept is already used at some places in Hyderabad. However, the implementation of this concept can lead to more traffic altogether, only better distributed over time.

The public display of the interviewees' opinions and suggestions as the ones described above in the Citizens' Exhibition offers unusual but attractive new roles for the participants. The expectations arising from this new role alone can be enough to motivate the actors to call on abilities which in many cases have been lying dormant. This leads to an empowerment experience. One of the effects of this is that the participants find themselves in the political process. In addition, the exhibition underlines their new role as representatives of their neighbourhood and of their political concern. They present themselves and their cause to the public. They are the hosts of the exhibition. The exhibits are portraits of internal views, needs, problems, political goals, concerning which they are the experts.

Furthermore, the Citizens' Exhibition has an important function in generating public interest. It provides a "stage" for the participatory process. The participants can exhibit their concerns here in public. That can have effects both internally and externally. The internal effects results from participants meeting one another and exchanging views, and the external effects result from the opportunities provided for the public to inform themselves about the issues and then to involve themselves in the process. Furthermore, by inviting political representatives and the press it is possible to achieve public impact beyond the immediate neighbourhood.

The visitors of the exhibition were asked to state their ideas and problems concerning traffic and transport in Hyderabad. The following selection of comments shall illustrate some of the prevalent opinions mentioned:

> *It's better people like us seriously start using cycle. I am starting from tomorrow. Right now I do it 2 times a week. From tomorrow I make it 7 times a week.* (IYCN 06/2009)

Road has remained same in size or marginally increased while number of vehicles has increased by 400%..?' (Tarnaka 02/2009)

I think it would be up to the youth to popularise the use of cycle to prevent it from being looked down upon. That would make it something like a fashion statement. (IYCN 06/2009)

Please walk for a distance within 3 km. It will be healthy rather than waste and generate fossil fuel by using a car. (IYCN 06/2009)

In Bangalore, empty autos (rickshaws) moving around are fined. They are supposed to park at auto stands and wait to get hired. In Hyderabad empty autos move at snail pace on busy roads and halt traffic and irritate ppl!!! (IYCN 06/2009)

In the following months it was shown at the 2nd Hyderabad Youth Summit on Climate Change (June $20^{th}/21^{st}$), the IGU Urban Commission Conference 'Emerging Urban Transformations: Multilayered Cities and Urban Systems (July 30th till August $9^{th})$, as well as on the premises of the Jawaharlal Nehru Technological University (JNTU) – School of Planning and Architecture, now Jawaharlal Nehru Architecture and Fine Arts University, JNAFAU, (August $10^{th} - 24^{th}$) in order to further foster the intense discourse on the topics discussed among the citizens involved.

3.2.3 Evaluation

The citizens' exhibition was very successful in its function of generating public interest for the issue of traffic and transportation in Hyderabad. The primary objective was to collect and present personal perspectives of citizens, players and group representatives on problems related to transport as well as their suggestions and visions to solve them. Apart from interviewing citizens from all walks of life, traffic police was also interviewed. The secondary objectives of the exhibition were to facilitate an increased understanding of the problematic issues among citizens, to spur public dialogue among the citizens and between citizens and the departments of official machinery responsible for these issues. The objectives could be commendably achieved through the aesthetic and emotional power of pictures with quotations, which is a major strength of this approach.

The evaluation of interviews has shown that the interviewees were well aware of different problems related to traffic and transportation in Hyderabad. However, they seemed to find no connection between the problems, situations in daily life and climate change. Though dissatisfaction was expressed about the public transportation system in particular and traffic in general, the immediate result of both "strong pollution" was scarcely mentioned in the interviews. Lack of safety on roads and inadequate public transportation system were the two main issues mentioned in the interviews. To improve safety on roads, zebra crossings and more traffic signals were suggested. Posting traffic police personnel at traffic signals to ensure that the traffic follows the signals correctly was also recommended. Teaching children in the school about traffic behaviour to improve traffic discipline was another valuable suggestion made. Extending the available Multi Modal Transport System (MMTS) and ensuring connectivity between MMTS and buses of the Andhra Pradesh Road Transport Corporation (APSRTC) were the two main propositions to improve the inadequate public transport system.

Through the public display of their views in the exhibition, the interviewees were ushered in to play an unusual but attractive role of representatives, which could ultimately lead them to be a part of the political process. The Citizens' exhibition therefore was a very positively perceived tool of participation; people were proud that they were part of it and friends and neighbours proud to recognise people shown in the exhibition. Also, many organisations (Alliance Française, Goethe Centre etc.) were very eager to show the exhibition in the course of other events dealing with climate change.

To improve this approach further and to make it result oriented, it became obvious that follow-up activities including the various suggestions of the participants to improve traffic and transportation in Hyderabad would be necessary to present the statements also to the representatives of concerned departments, political parties and NGOs. The traffic police which used to conduct programmes like "Traffic Safety Week" at regular intervals have discontinued them. Based on the results of the exhibition and further activities, they could be requested to restart such actions to raise public awareness for climate change and thereby motivate them to opt for climate friendly transport behaviour.

3.3 The Online-Dialogue

3.3.1 Method

The parallel online-dialogue, launched March and ended May, 31th 2009 was initially developed as part of the project's website and later on created as a discussion forum on the social internet networks "Facebook" and "Orkut"[7] to gain greater attention for the online-dialogue especially among the target group of young internet users. It was promoted via different channels of communication. The online discussion accompanied the participative method of the Citizens' Exhibition, which was inaugurated in Feb 2009 and shown on several premises all around the city if Hyderabad in order to foster the discourse on the traffic and transport issues.

The online-dialogue aims at activating as many citizens and actors from Hyderabad as possible to give their views and discuss about

1. *the problems they face with the prevailing traffic conditions in Hyderabad*
2. *their visions and ideas – according to their personal situation – for an ideal climate-friendly, energy efficient transport system in their neighbourhood or the city of Hyderabad in the year 2020 and*
3. *feasible solutions or action strategies for a more sustainable traffic system with lower emission levels*

which can be realised for their neighbourhood or the city of Hyderabad. The knowledge and the ideas generated in the online-dialogue shall be analysed and incorporated in future planning processes of the project. Invitations were distributed online as well as offline via the Goethe-Centre's and the different project-partners' mailing lists, workshop participants, universities and online groups such as APEC, Karmayog, and the social networks mentioned above. In addition to this, press releases in English and Telugu were sent to different newspapers in town to gain a wider spectrum of participants from around the city.

Even though the questions have been modified twice and the name was changed from "online-dialogue" to "online discussion forum" in advertisements (as online dialogue could lead to confusion), only a small amount of people reacted to the questions (30 answers online and 54 offline survey). An accompanying offline survey conducted in August 2009 on the campus of Osmania University and at events of the Goethe Centre, as well as on the streets of Hyderabad was able to deliver more statements and ideas related to the questions of traffic and transport in Hyderabad than the online-dialogue.

---

[7] Orkut and Facebook are international social networking websites. Orkut is mainly used in India but less in Europe, whereas Facebook is quite popular in India as well as in Europe.

3.3.2 Realisation

In the following paragraphs will be described how the participants reacted to the set of questions on problems associated with traffic and transport in Hyderabad. In the online-dialogue the following questions were asked:

Problems:

What are the problems you face moving around Hyderabad or your neighbourhood? - Please tell us about the most important obstacles and risks you (or any member of your family) experience in your everyday life while walking, driving or travelling.

Visions:

How would – according to your personal situation – the ideal sustainable traffic and transport system of the city or your neighbourhood look like in the future? Do you have any dreams, an idea or vision of your Hyderabad in the year 2020? Please think of your future vision of Hyderabad in the year 2020, taking into account your personal situation or the situation of your family.

Solutions:

What kind of solutions could you think of to improve the traffic and transport situation for you personally and regarding the reduction of CO_2-emissions in Hyderabad? What actions could be taken in your immediate neighbourhood? What can or would YOU personally do to make a change? Please make your proposals for concrete measures which could be implemented or essential actions to take and make suggestions who should take responsibility.

Problems associated with the traffic and transport situation in Hyderabad

The main problems we generally face in Hyderabad are traffic, accidents, pollution.
The overall problems mentioned can be put in order as follows: Traffic in general, pedestrian safety, driving behaviour (of private drivers) and environment/pollution issues in Hyderabad seem to be the most frequent problems people have to deal with. Following, they named the infrastructure (traffic system), public transportation issues, construction work, the failure of government, public responsibility and others such as problems of the hawkers, parking and cyclists.

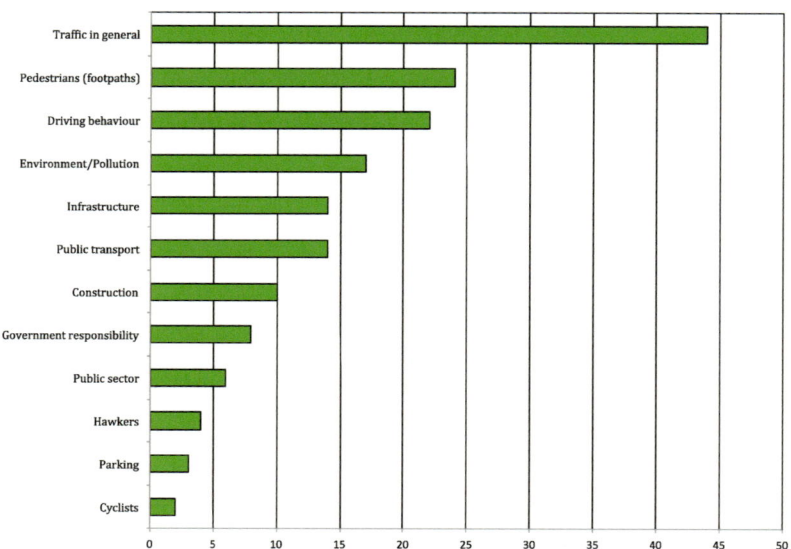

Figure 4: Categories of the problems mentioned

Traffic in general

The traffic in Hyderabad is definitely one of the worst in the world.
Traffic jams due to heavy traffic and road accidents are frequently mentioned as major problems of the city. The interviewees blame the inadequate work done by government agencies for this lack of traffic flow and high rate of accidents. It is mentioned that the road system has not been planned or worked out strategically.

"The worst part of Hyderabad is Traffic! Because of the continuous digging on the roads for pipelines etc, there's a lot of problem and littering on the roads".
In this remark it can be seen, that the road construction for an improvement of the city's infrastructure (be it pipelines or road improvement) is experienced as a major source of inconvenient traffic flow. The traffic police do not seem to be able to deal with their challenges of a growing traffic in Hyderabad. On the contrary, they are blamed to add to the chaotic traffic situation. One citizen describes the traffic police of Hyderabad as being *"probably the worst traffic police in the country. Most of these Policemen are too young and frail to be of an effective law enforcement."*
Another stated: *"The traffic police is totally incompetent and only interested in collecting some penalty amount from smaller offenders and letting the bigger offenders scold – free".*

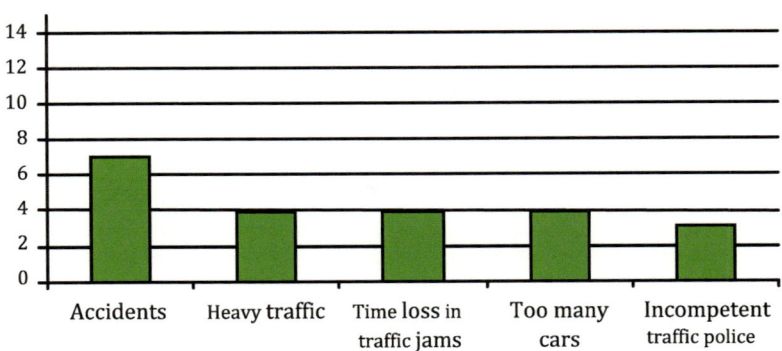

Figure 5: Problems stated to traffic in general

Pedestrian safety

The problems related to pedestrian safety – the *"Lack of pedestrian pathways"* has been mentioned quite frequently. Several interviewees felt that there is no safety for pedestrians at all, due to the absence of footpaths and the encroachment of the latter. Nonetheless, the encroachment of hawkers has not been mentioned as often as expected. In the course of the workshops and conferences held in Feb 2009 this issue came up frequently but was not uttered to the same extent by the participants of the online-dialogue. More important are problems related to the footpath-road-ratio. Problems such as *"no proper pedestrian crossing (...) no safety for pedestrians"* or *"(...) there are no footpaths and therefore no place for people to walk, parking place is inadequate"* are voiced quite often. Lacking is in general space for pedestrians to walk freely and safely in particular. An omnipresent shortage of zebra crossings and pedestrian bridges all around the city has been mentioned a couple of times:

"Main ache is wasting lots of time due to traffic and roads are so small and more foot-over bridges should be done (...)"

Even though the lack of footpaths is a phenomenon which can be seen all over India, the existence of an Hyderabad-based NGO called *Right to Walk Foundation* also points out this problem of the pedestrians as a particular one in Hyderabad.

The problem of cycling being too dangerous and therefore not preferable to travel around the city is also mentioned in several comments. As the roads are too crowded and too poorly maintained, cycling is not a real option to the commuters. Going by (motor) bike is assumed to be a safer and quicker means of transportation.

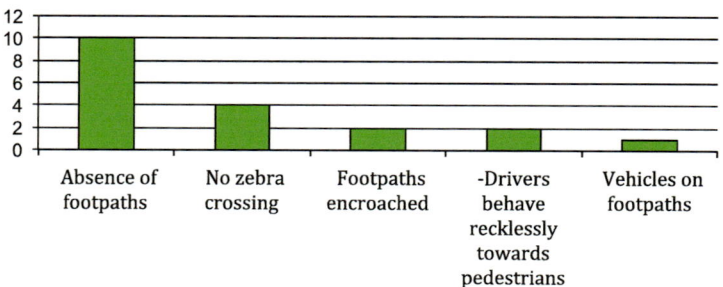

Figure 6: Problems stated relating to pedestrian safety

Private drivers

The problem of the very disturbing driving behaviour is another overall problem stated quite often.

> *Hyderabad is very nice place to live but the lack of traffic awareness in the public and the poor maintenance of the road system also causing a tough time for all the vehicle drivers. Hyderabad city is really in need to be upgraded. Nowadays the city came up with lots of flyovers in the busy areas which are also not properly used by everyone. The common cause of heavy traffic is breaking the traffic rules all over the city by almost everyone. Also it's become mandatory for us unless we break traffic rules we cannot reach our destination soon.*

Even though attaining a driver's licence is mandatory, many people do not tend to follow this rule. The result is an often reckless driving attitude. One citizen made the following statement blaming the citizens themselves for the bad traffic situation in the city:

> *The public of Hyderabad is to be blamed for this or any inconvenience in transportation. They don't handle public transport provided by the government carefully nor follow traffic rules, any rules rather. They ride their vehicles as if it's their dad's road. In fact I've seen people have 'It's ma dad's road' written on the back. Everyone is in his own hurry and wants to go first, which is the main cause for all of this chaos. All they do is blame the government for all the upset. So the public has to be straightened, until then, they deserve such uncomfortable traffic situations.'*

But the overall lack of traffic awareness described is also due to the traffic police's behaviour, which is criticised as well. It was cited that many police men are not properly trained and therefore do not seem to make an impression of being capable of dealing with the challenge of constantly rising aggressive driving attitudes and lacking driving skills. *("If reposted, the police have a very passive attitude".)* This problem can partly be attributed to the fact that many drivers on Hyderabad's streets do not own a driver's license at all. (*"Rash driving without a driving licence"*).

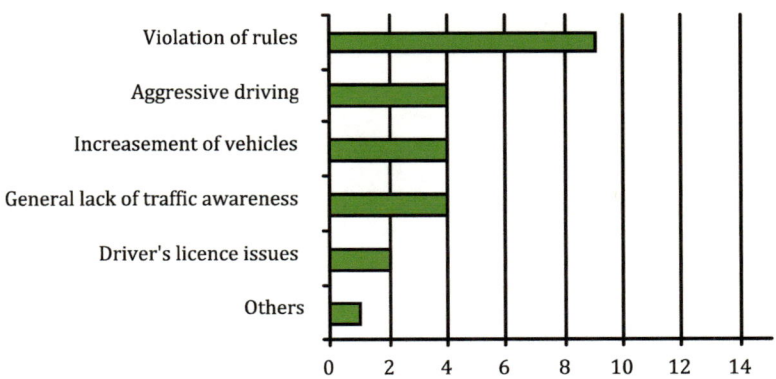

Figure 7: Problems stated relating to private drivers

Infrastructure

In addition to this, the general (bad) infrastructure of the city was also pointed out to cause many problems. That is in particular: footpaths, not maintained roads, too narrow roads and others, such as lack of bike lanes, too many cables hanging, inadequate parking etc.

The absence of footpaths, which is also represented in the pedestrian safety - category and the poor maintained road system (with too narrow roads) are the most cited problems of the citizens. This unorganised image of the city may lead to a situation where the people of Hyderabad do not trust their authorities anymore. Someone uttered following statement:

"Around Hyderabad the traffic is more and the roads are small. There is no certain plan for roads that's why there are traffic jams".

Another citizen:

The percentage of road space is far too less compared to the area of Hyderabad city, now Greater Hyderabad. The Public Transport system is grossly inadequate and hence everyone wants to have their own vehicle. There are too many two, three and four wheelers on the road. Hyderabadis do not follow any traffic rules and put their own lives and the lives of others, especially pedestrians' lives, in danger. (...).

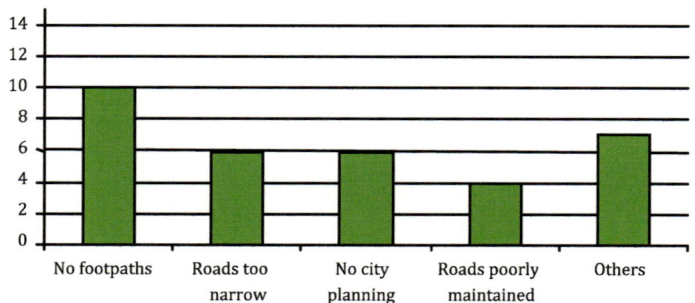

Figure 8: Problems stated relating to infrastructure

Public Transport

Concerning the public transportation system there were also not as many statements made as expected in the first place. Nonetheless some comments can be presented to show the major problems of the citizens. *"The major problem we face in our daily life is travelling around the city 'cause there is a lack of buses and as a result they are crowded which cause inconvenience."*

Buses are too crowded, uncomfortable and unreliable. The transport system is named to be just too inefficient. The lack of connectivity between railway and other modes of transportation is unexpectedly not really an issue among the interviewees – only one mentioned that. People tend to be more focussed on private driving and do not seem to see public transport as a real option. This is also due to the very unsafe situation many people face while commuting in public transportation. Many people need to shift from public transport to auto-rickshaws, which are more costly and also not always the safer alternative – one said: *"the autowallahs [driver of an auto-rickshaw] are careless"*.

All in all – the traffic situation is again most challenging for the ones who cannot afford to have their own driver or car – but even then, the reckless driving behaviour of everyone (else) puts the traffic participants in danger.

Environment

Several statements were made concerning environmental issues and pollution in the city.

14 participants named pollution in general (11) and noise pollution in particular (3) as a major source of problems. The term pollution is manifold and includes pollution of air, water and soil, noise, light, thermal and visual pollution as well as insufficient waste disposal - littering.

Littering is also a problem of many Indian urban structures. However one participant stated: *"Lack of garbage bins – hence all the commercial and household waste is spread on the roads."* This waste pollution is also another aspect which adds up to the chaotic impression of the city. Again it can be said that the authorities are being (implicitly) blamed for this situation by the participants of this online-discussion. Even though efforts have been made to make Hyderabad a clean city, the lack of an efficient garbage disposal system is quite obvious. Another major problem citizens mentioned is the lack of greenery all over the city. As more and more areas are extended, the green spaces vanish.

Visions of the citizens regarding a future scenario of Hyderabad

In the course of gathering visions of citizens, the citizens were asked to express ideas towards a sustainable scenario in 2020 concerning their personal situation; the ideal traffic and transport system or the neighbourhood. They were asked to mention their dreams for Hyderabad in 2020.

Regarding those citizens' visions for Hyderabad in the year 2020, there are rather negative than positive views. Many utterances on the general situation of Hyderabad in the future were quite negative. Sixteen said that the situation will become worse, more congested and dangerous as the number of cars will increase. It is assumed that by more and more traffic to come, the situation for pedestrians will become even more unbearable. Below some quotes that shall illustrate the views of the citizens:

> *In future Hyderabad looks really congested and dangerous as the no. of automobiles may go higher and as in future the mass and public transportation looks like a failure as many are buying private vehicles.* These participants see Hyderabad in 2020 as *a haphazardly grown city with decentralised CBDs and working zones, making it even more difficult and dangerous to travel.*
>
> *It may or will be a busy city with lots of traffic with hardly any walking space*

By 2020 the traffic is going to become worse

We will leave the place and will move to another location

Full of traffic, scarcity of water

If not controlled, it will result in more traffic jams and accidents

It would be the most polluted city in India?

(...) If this is the situation now and no authorities are taking action, there will be a day when you can not even find footpaths on the roads as even the footpaths will be filled with vehicles. The local buses, though they are the cheaper way of transport, they will mainly cause traffic jams

Areas where the rich live will have wider and greener roads and all the waste would be dumped in the areas of the weaker sections

If no corrective measures are taken starting now – everything will turn out of control. It is frightening to imagine the future of Hyderabad at this present state of change (...)

Given the present state of affairs, possibly worse than what it is now especially with new cars Nano and more spending power. I would like to see more pavements, cycle lanes, no motorised vehicles on some streets and a proper public transport system. Is that too much? Above all I would like to see politicians and Govt authorities working for the public and not only for self kudos.

12 million pollution (population), skyscrapers, pollution, metro transportation, muss lesser civic sense than our present day scenario etc., less available space for living, congested lanes, by lanes disappearing natural beauty

Ten interviewees mentioned positive ideas for a future Hyderabad. These included an eco-friendly vehicular system, clean roads, enough parking space, reliable public transport system and enough bridges and flyovers to clean the roads of traffic.

In 2020, Hyderabad will have clean roads and so many bridges and flyovers will develop the traffic jams clean. The metro rail is to begin in the future vision.

Another one mentioned the metro as a positive future traffic vision saying:

I think technology will be improved so the traffic will not be a problem in future

Eco-friendly and well aesthetic view for Hyderabad and more usage of public transportation in the city

One even predicted: *"In the year 2020, Hyderabad is one of the role model cit[ies] in India"*.

Only a single citizens advanced a rather careful opinion saying that it will all remain the same in the future saying: *"I think the present scenario will remain same even after 11 years in 2020"*.

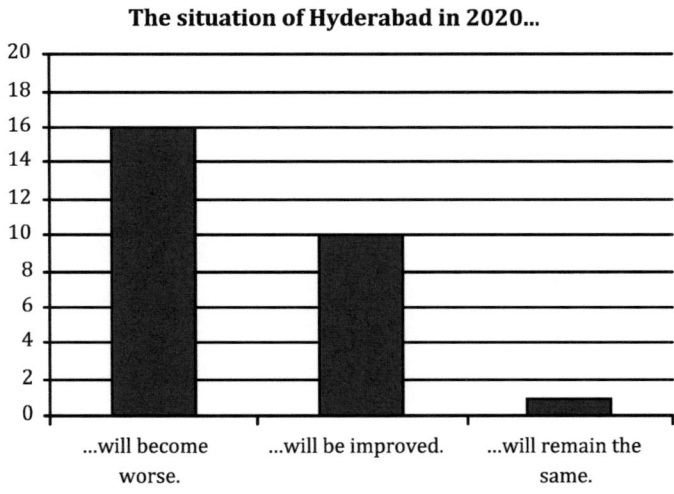

Figure 9: Future Scenario

Solutions proposed

Put more emphasis on improving mass (public) transport system, provide barrier free footpath, plant more trees along roads, reduction on use of petrol and diesel.

The uttered solutions can be categorised as following - traffic surveillance, infrastructure, public transport, public awareness, technical aspects, and environment. Summing up the different categories of solutions, two citizens stated:

The number of personal vehicles on the road everyday has to be brought down. That is possible only with an efficient public transport system. That will reduce CO_2 emission. That will reduce pollution. Footpaths must be made on every road. Every citizen should be given the right to walk safely. Footpaths should be clean and kept free for pedestrians to walk on.

1. Traffic surveillance and regulation is required at unmanned / unautomated traffic signal points. E.g. Secunderabad Club, Electric Substation Junction Trimulgherry.

2. Dividers at main roads, with facility of u-turn at correct junction should be provided. This will bring more traffic discipline and also not inconvenience travellers.

3. Errant drivers and those flouting rules should be held and fined heavily, if not at one point then through wireless. The errant drivers should be relentlessly pursued and fined.

4. Mobile traffic grievance vans should be established by traffic police to listen to complaints of wrong or fast driving or road rage. I do not know where to complain, so what should I do?

5. As a citizen I follow traffic rules, do not overtake from wrong side, follow traffic line in narrow road and expect the same from everybody.

6. Regular demonstrations should be organised area wise to highlight traffic rules and why they must not be flouted. NOTHING IS MORE PRECIOUS THAN HUMAN LIFE!!! EVERYTHING ELSE CAN WAIT, BE SLOW BE SAFE

Better traffic surveillance as a solution

Solutions concerning *traffic surveillance* were the ones most eagerly mentioned. The most often expressed solution is the implementation of stricter traffic rules like a prohibition of eating and using cell phones while driving. A reduction of cars in general and old and noisy cars in particular is claimed. Cars should be reduced by law or other disincentives - for example by making it obligatory for every household to have only a specific amount of cars *("implementation of law for maximum no.'s of cars and vehicles per family")* or by making *"fuel-consuming SUVs unaffordable even for the rich by heavy taxing for use."* A ban on all old cars and a *"restriction of buses or heavy vehicles within the neighbourhoods"* is also claimed.

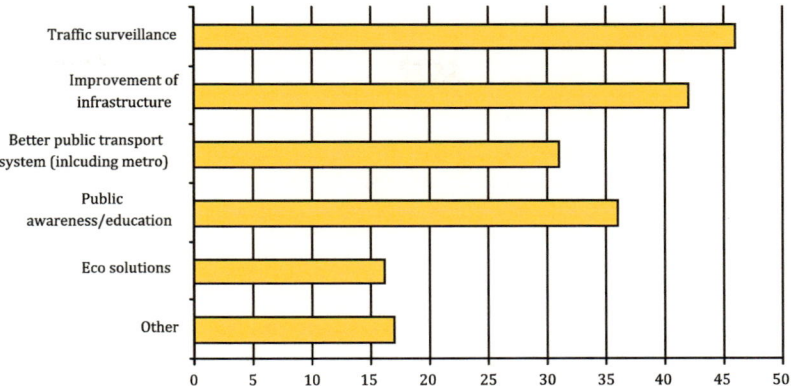

Figure 10: Overview of the solutions mentioned

One interviewee named his six solutions to the current problems of the city:

1. Strict pollution checks for all vehicles 2. Use of C.N.G.[8] for public transport 3. Discarding of aged vehicles 4. Strict punishments to offenders. 5. Good licence issuing practice and issuing tickets to offenders 6. Use of Euro 5 standard vehicles

Furthermore applying stricter rules and regulations for obtaining a driver's licence were stated. *"Every vehicle owner should opt for the time, route etc., while taking the driving license. The driving license card should denote the time, route etc. If the vehicle is driven other than the time, route etc., the driver of the vehicle should be penalised with say Rs.1,000"* – uttered as a feasible solution. Besides, a satellite controlled traffic signal system is claimed once. *"Traffic surveillance and regulation is required at unmanned / unautomated traffic signal points. E.g. Secunderabad Club (...)"*.

As another innovative idea, a law or an extra tax on the usage of private cars – according to the number of days used is called for (*"implementation of law for maximum no.'s of cars and vehicles per family/ I would definitely follow the above"*).

Solutions concerning infrastructure

Following, ideas concerning the inefficient infrastructure of the city are described.

---

[8] CNG – Compressed Natural Gas. It is a substitute for petrol, diesel, or propane fuel. Although it also does produce greenhouse gases, it is a more environmentally clean alternative to those fuels. CNG has been made party compulsory to public transportation in India (e.g. Delhi).

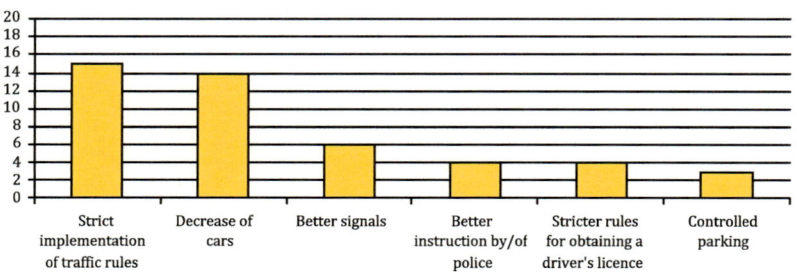

Figure 11: Solutions mentioned concerning traffic surveillance

Concerning the infrastructure of the city, flyovers and bridges were most often named as traffic obstacles most desired to be solved. Also quite important seems to be the road- and footpath improvement as well as the establishment of a bicycle lane system in the most connected parts of the city. The construction work should be finished until the monsoon starts, so that the construction sites will not make the chaos on the streets worse. Separate lanes for buses, cars and pedestrians, as well as zebra crossings were claimed to be introduced. Further solutions include dividers/road medians at main roads making it more clear where to turn and dangerous road shortcuts impossible, as well as moving back of the stop lines (at crossings) instead of having the zebra crossing right where the cars stop in front of the lights.

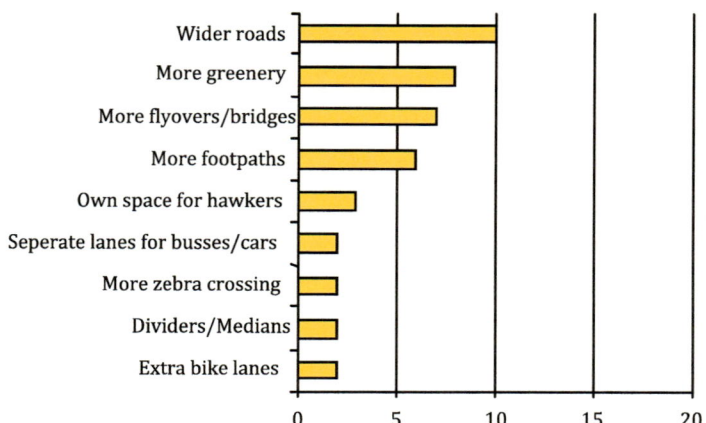

Figure 12: Solutions mentioned concerning an improved infrastructure

Solutions regarding public awareness

As another feasible solution the aspect of public awareness is mentioned. If people are not willing to change their behaviour, there is not much to do from the planning authorities.

That shall include education and training programmes on traffic and pollution issues as well as mass-encouragement of bicycles.

"Educate people. Common sense has to be taught to people. It's a disgrace. Every educational institution should take monthly classes on these issues showing/focusing reality".

In this course, regular demonstrations stressing the importance of traffic rules are mentioned as well as training classes and distribution of gloves and helmets for cyclist. Interestingly, a publicity campaign with (Bollywood -) celebrities was suggested to further foster the public awareness-efforts in India/Hyderabad. Thus one statement was made saying:

> *(...) but, especially in Hyderabad, we see how stars can influence people's behaviour. if a few of the big Tollywood heroes would make this king (d) of progressive publicity, and traffic police be instructed in the right way, maybe more people could ride their bicycle"*.

Solutions concerning public transportation

The public transport system shall be enhanced. This means in particular a better encouragement of the public transport and an improvement of the latter. The metro project is to be started and the number of buses and the MMTS service to be increased. There is a need to be better connectivity between trains and buses.

One statement claims that *"the public transport has to become energy-efficient in itself (use of CNG gas). The government should take responsibilities to increase more public and mass transportation system like electric trains, buses, metros etc. which discourage private transportation and so their emission of CO_2"*.

3.3.3 Evaluation of the Method

Among the citizens of Hyderabad online-dialogue was not accepted to the same extent as face-to-face communication. Unfortunately, despite the actual growth of the internet usage in India, there has been an immense lack of participation in the online-participation that has to be considered closely before analysing the findings of this tool.

It has to be considered, that the majority of the Indian population does not have a (proper) access to the internet.[9] This is mainly due to a lack of infrastructure but also to a lacking awareness (on how to use the internet) among the majority of people. Therefore highly engaged target groups such as the age group 50+ or people living below the poverty line, suffering the most in the course of the pollution, cannot be addressed properly via the WWW. As could be seen on Facebook and Orkut – many people (130 members on Facebook) wanted to be a part of the group "Towards climate & citizen friendly transport & traffic solutions Hyderabad", but still did not answer any questions or express any opinion. The internet seems to be first and foremost used as an entertainment or social networking tool, not a tool of participation or discussion. The lack of opinion leader participating in the discussion forum might have added to the problem of online participation; it is very difficult to gain attention of the broad public.

The discussion platform being only in English might add to this problem as people who are not perfectly fluent in written English might get discouraged by having to answer only in a foreign language. In addition, the website's design might be too neutral compared to Indian websites. The highly anonymous approach of this online tool might not be an adequate one for the Indian culture, which is closely linked to interpersonal relations. It has to be also stated that the category on visions was sometimes misunderstood and used to further express solutions rather than future visions of what kind of place Hyderabad will become in the future. To use these comments on solutions mentioned nonetheless, the visions that were more of a solution, were subsequently used as such. However, some statements could be collected that may help to formulate ideas based on the citizens' statements for a better traffic and transport system in Hyderabad.

In this context it also has to be mentioned again, that the Indian middle class, that may want to have their say in the topics discussed, might not be properly addressed by this online-tool of participation. The people, who were addressed personally in the course of the offline survey on the campus of Osmania University, were very eager to answer the questions most sincerely. Regrettably, most of the interviewees were not willing to go online to do so in the same extent. There has also been some feedback saying that the answers requested in detail might discourage the participants as it is too time-consuming. A multiple choice survey might be more attractive as people are more used to multiple choice questionnaires. Summing up, the socio-cultural aspect has to be

---

[9] "At present, only about one in 10 Indians, or about 100 million people, use the internet on a regular basis" (http://news.bbc.co.uk/2/hi/business/8067930.stm 08.12.2009).

closely considered as the online-dialogue does at this time not appear to be an efficient tool of participation for the Indian context.

Analysis of Responses

The problems mentioned were related to traffic in general and the increase of vehicles as well as incompetent traffic authorities in particular. The overall absence of footpaths as a result of an inefficient city planning was an issue most frequently stated. Rules and regulations are not followed – which is not only due to the already mentioned incompetence of the authorities but also to a general lacking social sense within the traffic participants. Signals are skipped, pedestrians threatened and roads misused as multiple lane sections which all add up to a quite chaotic situation in the streets of Hyderabad. Stated solutions for these omnipresent problems were therefore mostly related to traffic surveillance. That includes a stricter implementation of traffic rules and calls for more action of the police. An overall decrease of cars was also claimed. It has to be kept in mind that as soon as the spread of small and cheap cars will be intensified, it will be soon resulting in a further increase of cars instead. Therefore this uttered solution seems to be a noble but a fairly unrealistic one as well. The Indian public is obviously willing to use more cars than already existing.

To ridden the streets of an overflow of cars, the only option seems to be an improvement of the public transport system. As many citizens describe the present state of public transportation in Hyderabad as unreliable, insufficient, overcrowded and therefore highly uncomfortable, there is no stimulus for the citizens to use public transportation instead of their private vehicles. Hence, the number of buses has to be increased and new options of public transportation are to be created. The Metro is mentioned a couple of times as a positive as well as a negative option (*"No Metro please!"*) which shows the highly ambivalent public opinion on that matter. The MMTS service is also called to be extended. Generally spoken, the citizens who participated would shift to a more sustainable public transport usage if there were appealing options – but that also calls for the authorities to act upon these claims.

As another major solution the improvement of the overall infrastructure is mentioned. That includes wider roads, more greenery, flyovers, footpaths, zebra crossings as well as allotted spaces for hawkers. Furthermore, citizens mentioned a separate lane system (taking Delhi as an example) for buses, cars and bicycles to lessen the irritation constantly arising as buses, cars, motorbikes and bicycles and pedestrians as well have to share the roads.

These ideas are not all aiming at a complete restructuring of the existing infrastructure. Many participants try to find small adjustments that have to be made in order to make the city safer for the citizens. Nonetheless, it has to be kept in mind, that a mere change of surroundings (wider streets etc) does not necessarily solve the problems lying within society. The education and awareness of the masses seems to be the biggest challenge as large-scale changes of the city can only be made with the help of the inhabitants. If the streets are widened but still not used properly, the improvement that was once expected might fail to appear. The authorities are therefore urged to invest in proper training of their law-enforcing services as well as in educating everyone who is using the streets.

3.4 Citizens' Charter for Urban Transport

3.4.1 Method

As an effort to make public service providers more open and accountable, the Government of India launched the quite ambitious "Citizen's Charter"[10] initiative both in central and state government departments in 1997. The Department of Administrative Reforms and Public Grievances (DARPG) stated in one of its publications on that topic:

> *It has been recognised world over that good governance is essential for sustainable development, both economic and social. The three essential aspects emphasised in good governance are transparency, accountability and responsiveness of the administration. "Citizens' Charters" initiative is a response to the quest for solving the problems which a citizen encounters, day in and day out, while dealing with the organisations providing public services. (Ministry of Personnel, Public Grievances and Pensions, Department of Administrative Reforms and Public Grievances 2003)*

3.4.2 Realisation

The conference on "Hyderabad Citizens' Charter for Urban Transport" was held in addition to the Citizens' Exhibition on February, 21st 2009. It was jointly organised

---

[10] Originally formulated was the objective of a Citizens' Charter by the British Government of John Major in 1991 as a national program. The original aim was to improve the quality of public services for the people of the country so that these services respond to the needs and wishes of the users. The program was relaunched in 1998 by the Labour Government of Tony Blair which rechristened it "Services First".

with the Goethe-Centre Hyderabad, the Hyderabad-based Right to Walk Foundation and PTV/Germany.

Figure 13: l: Speakers at the conference for a Citizens' Charter for Urban Transport; r: Audience at the conference for a Citizens' Charter for Urban Transport

The conference's aim was to bring together the most important stakeholders from different levels in the field of transport and traffic in order to discuss the different interests and possible conflicts and to eventually formulate a charter for citizen-friendly traffic. About 60 - 80 participants and speakers from various civil society organisations, professional organisations, transport corporations, government offices and universities took part in the conference. Mrs. Chandana Chakrabarti, an active voice in the city, and member of *Medically Aware Responsible Citizens of Hyderabad* (MARCH) moderated the Forum.

Speakers and topics were:

1. Mrs. Kanti Kannan, president of Right to Walk Foundation: 5 steps to make the city pedestrian friendly
2. Mr. M. Vedakumar, Forum for Better Hyderabad: Key issues of Hyderabad in a nutshell
3. Prof. Lakshmana Rao, Head of Transport Department, JNTU: Visions of traffic and transport: 2020
4. Prof. C. Ramachandraiah, Citizens for Better Public Transport in Hyderabad (CBPTH): Metro: how, when and where?
5. Mr. Georg Kern, PTV: German example of charter's implementation – city of Nuremberg

6. Mr. K. Vijayaraghavar, MMTS Travellers Group: Suggested improvements in MMTS. Phase 1/Phase 2.

7. Mr. Kishore, APSRTC: 5 steps to a better bus public transport system

8. Mr. Prasanna Desai, architect, Pune: Is BRTS the answer to Indian cities?

9. Mr. Bojja from Hyderabad Metropolitan Development Authority (HMDA): Hyderabad has grown out of proportions. Resulted in Cyberabad.

10. Prof. Günter Nest, regional planner, Kunsthochschule Weißensee: What we should not lose in the Indian street.

11. Mr. Shankar Narayan; architect: Busting the peak hours and some other ideas.

12. Mr. V. S. Rao, State President of the APSRTC Staff and Workers Federation: Difficulties and suggestions for driving a bus in the city.

13. Mr. Randhadir Reddy, South Central Railway: How much more can railways contribute to the city's urban transport needs?

The conference was organised as a lecture – discussion forum. The presented lectures on pedestrian safety, city planning and traffic and transport were subsequently followed by a vivid discussion among the participants. The discussions and presentations were very vibrant and showed a high understanding of the problems' complexity. Mrs. Kanti Kannan, the first speaker of the day, presented her vision of a pedestrian friendly city. She mentioned several disturbing problems pedestrians have to face in Hyderabad:

> *Lot of cheap two wheelers are there but no sidewalks. The weak suffer. Five pedestrians die every week in Hyderabad. (...) What is being done against the encroachment of footpaths? Officials need to walk on footpaths. If they walk, things will change. Clear the footpaths (...). Make footpaths not accessible to motorcycles. Sanitation: Proper toilets are needed. Even the Commissioner should be able to use the public toilets. Relocate the transformers. Footpaths should have adequate width. (...) .*

Concerning the pressing need of establishing new public transportation modes it was said, that the MMTS system, comparable to the German S-Bahn, is a most convenient way of travelling around the city. A speaker stated that regrettably the city authorities do not really bother about improving the already existing system, which would be more cost-effective than the planned metro. He suggested: *"160 km railway track capacity is available. With 350 crores the city will have a good MMTS system."*

Another speaker suggested taking the in Delhi introduced Bus Rapid Transport System (BRTS) as an example to improve the traffic system in Hyderabad. *"BRTS is the system needed not metro rail. (...) The use of private vehicles should be discouraged."* Shankar Narayan, Hyderabad-based architect suggested establishing a new system of traffic:

> *Urban traffic flows are time based, daily cyclical, predictable, peak and off-peak and are heavily directional. Staggered planning has to be done. Different parts of the city should have different timings. Staggered working hours. Dynamic medians are needed.*

The participants then reacted with vivid participation, some agreeing with the stated ideas and utterances, some disagreeing and voicing their own problems and demands such as:

> *...signals do not work. Corruption plays the spoil. Malls are allowed to be built where they are not supposed to be built.*

> *Nowhere it is thought of to include the citizens in decision making. We have to grab our position/right.*

> *Tamil Nadu and Andhra Pradesh are the leaders in losing lives.*

3.4.3 Evaluation

The conference showed that, although the awareness of Indian people for the issue of climate change is rising according to recent polls, the traffic problem is not perceived primarily as an environmental or energy problem, but rather as a safety (e.g. low safety for pedestrians and too many accidents due to the disobeying of traffic rules, missing pedestrian crossings and footpaths, obstruction of footpaths by street vendors) and time problem (long commuting times due to an inadequate public transportation system and traffic jams). In addition, some of the citizens demanded for a directly elected Mayor with executive powers for Hyderabad. The citizens' demands were subsequently handed over to politicians of Hyderabad.

Unfortunately, there are several problems that may occur in implementing a citizens' charter. As the above mentioned Handbook states, an introduction of a new concept is always quite difficult in any organisation. Therefore, introduction and implementation of the concept of Citizens' Charters in India was much more difficult due to the old bureaucratic set up/ procedures and the rigid attitudes of the work force.

Box 1: Main demands mentioned

Summary of the citizens' demands:
1. Have a pedestrian policy, pedestrian policing
2. Zero tolerance for footpath encroachment, remove obstructions; transformers, trees, planters etc. by making semi-public zones for public convenience
3. Make special hawking zones
4. Pedestrian crossings to be provided
5. Regular audit of safety, security, risk and land use
6. Have a hierarchy of road system
7. Use GPS for violation
8. Increase utility of roads, mere widening of roads will not help
9. Increasing major junctions, mapping and controlling land use
10. Press for MMTS-II which has been approved in 2004
11. Bring urban transport into agenda of political parties
12. Prioritise lanes for buses in the city
13. Bring traffic education into school syllabi
14. Standardise speed breakers
15. Change design of buses to increase travelling space
16. BRTS is the viable solution which takes care not of transporting people but also of pedestrians and cyclists
17. Focus on moving people and not moving vehicles
18. Strengthen MMTS as it is now, implement MMTS-II, what we require is a comprehensive master plan of Hyderabad
19. Stagger timings of schools, shops and work
20. Have mobile medians instead of fixed medians
21. Shift traffic signals to more suitable position
22. Peak hours – allow cars but levy taxes for that
23. Levy high taxes on molls
24. Radial roads from the outer ring road into the city
25. Improve the driving license system
26. Formal training system for auto rickshaws

Most important, the mother of all agenda is here which is to have a Mayor who is directly elected by the citizens of the city: "Can we conduct an all party meeting demanding their views on the issue of directly elected mayor with executive powers for Hyderabad city – What is your response? What is everybody's response?"
YES in one voice!

The city of Hyderabad has multifarious traffic problems. These problems under which all sections of the society suffer are a matter of great concern in terms of climate change.

Besides causing high pollution, tremendous amounts of CO_2 are emitted into the atmosphere through the traffic chaos in the city, which could be reduced considerably through streamlining the traffic and improving the public transport system (PTS). If the PTS is improved, definitely more citizens who are now using personal vehicles will avail the facility. Though the situation is so grave, no effective initiatives are undertaken to study the problems systematically to find solutions for the obvious reason that no single stakeholder feels responsible for the problems. The PTS in Hyderabad consists of rail and road transport wings which are operated by two different organisations. The buses are operated by the state run APSRTC and the MMTS is operated by the Indian Railways. They are operated independently by both the organisations with practically no coordination.

Our preliminary observations of the traffic and transport situation in Hyderabad and the information collected through interviews of the Citizens' Exhibition have prompted us to initiate the "Hyderabad Citizens' Charter for Urban Transport". The conference was held in the first place to bring together the important stakeholders to sit together at one table to discuss about the prevailing problems, citizens' interests, possible conflicts and at the end to formulate a citizens' charter. As citizens took part in the conference, the representatives of the transport organisations also had the unique possibility to hear their problems, suggestions and visions and answer their questions.

Twelve speakers from different stakeholder organisations and experts gave lectures in the conference; each lecture was followed by a lively and fruitful discussion. The outcome at the end of the day was a well formulated charter of 26 demands.

In the conference, as it was the case with Citizens' Exhibition, the traffic problem was not perceived primarily as an environmental or an energy problem by the citizens who attended it, but rather as a problem of safety and responsibilities. All participants demanded with one voice that Hyderabad should have a directly elected Mayor with executive powers, who is responsible to the people. The idea behind this demand is that the Mayor as the apex and sole authority in the city would be responsible for the proper maintenance of all public amenities in the city and could coordinate the operations effectively e.g. in case of emergencies.

The conference was very appreciated by the public and the local stakeholders. In the end, the charter was handed over to politicians, but it is difficult to assess if the citizens' demands and ideas are made use of in any way (because bottom-up approaches are not always supported). Though, the implementation of the citizens' charter remains a distant goal. It is now left to the government and authorities concerned how seriously they take the charter and how it gets implemented. To ensure awareness of the main problems and to foster follow-up activities from the political level, an expert workshop has been planned in cooperation with all stakeholders of the Citizens' Charter Conference.

Some hope is in sight, as recently the Railway Board of the Indian Railways has cleared the MMTS phase II project for Hyderabad which was one of the demands in the charter. It will be implemented jointly by the State government and the South Central Railway (SCR) to expand the suburban railway network by another 107 km. (The Hindu 2010)

4 Conclusion: Impact & Sustainability

The measures undertaken showed that the inhabitants of Hyderabad are aware of the general problems of traffic and transportation when they get the opportunity to express their opinion. The personal focus mostly lies on local problems like traffic jams, pollution and noise and only to a small extent on global climate change and subsequent mitigation strategies. Furthermore there exist several civil society organisations in Hyderabad. They are active in very different concerns, but they have in common that they are aiming at fundamental improvements for a majority of the population.

On the other hand urban policy in Hyderabad is mostly based on large-scale and capital intensive projects such as the metro, flyovers, the Outer Ring Road, the airport etc. The overarching problem of these projects is that they are marginal reaching the poor urban population and do not fit to their requirements. This development will not lead to sustainability while preferring a numerical minority and not considering a socially deprived majority

Therefore, the participative processes and envisaged projects regarding a pedestrian policy and a better walkability for Hyderabad call for two levels of awareness raising and capacity building: The first is the policy and implementation level where decision makers and planners need to gain knowledge of the positive effects of walking. Consequently, administration has to integrate that knowledge into their working routines and argumentation: cost efficient mode of transport, vitally important for the poorer groups of society, reduction of energy-use, reduction of CO_2 emissions, good for health etc. Furthermore the importance of an attractive walking infrastructure for integrated and intermodal transport planning with the effect of an increased use of public transport has to be stressed. On the second level, public awareness has to be raised and increased and the positive effects for the individual have to be communicated (low-cost transport and health) together with advice how to make the way through the city by walking and public transport. The improvement of the situation for pedestrians has a strong focus on the social dimension as it supports the needs of 40 to 50 % of the citizens who have no other choice than to walk. It also includes a strong aspect of public health, as on an average 5 pedestrians are killed and 40 are injured every week[11]. At the same time it stabilises the financial situation for those dependent on walking as they do not have to switch to (and pay for) public transport. Moreover, the financial situation of the city can partly be released because the pressure on the roads may not increase that fast and therefore the building of flyovers and road-widening can be put on hold and instead an effective public transport system can come in place. Last but not least the project also has a strong focus on the ecologic dimension: as walking is the most environmentally sound and energy efficient mode of transport it is the aim of the project to keep the rate of pedestrians at least constant. In consequence the pace of motorisation – mostly two-wheelers – will decrease.

One important aspect has to be taken into account and future planning: As the metro system will be built within the next years, it is necessary to introduce a feasible footpath system as well to support the usability of the overall public transport system.

All of these aspects mentioned are part of an integrated urban planning. This means sustainable economic progress and improvements in quality of living at the same time, but for the entire population. For instance, public transport does not only lead to a mitigation of CO_2 emissions and less traffic jams, it also offers a cheap transport mode for people without own motorised vehicles.

The latest developments in Hyderabad showed that a growing interest for comprehensive urban planning exists also at the administrative level. The GHMC introduced a special cell for pedestrian issues and R2W investigated the first newly built stretches of footpaths. To ensure an ongoing process towards a liveable and walkable city of Hyderabad the fixed implementation of participatory procedures on the local level constitutes an essential condition.

---

[11] Statistics by A.P. Traffic police for the year 2006-2007.

References

Böhm, Birgit; Dienel, Hans-Liudger; Legewie, Heiner. 2008. Die Bürgerausstellung: Eine Kombination sozialwissenschaftlicher, partizipativer und künstlerischer Elemente. *Forum Qualitative Sozialforschung/Forum: Qualitative Social Research* 9(2) Art. 33.

Böhm, Birgit; Dienel, Hans-Liudger; Keppler, Dorothee; Legewie, Heiner (eds.). (not yet published). *Die Bürgerausstellung. Die Perspektive von Bürgern und Bürgerinnen als Gegenstand qualitativer Sozialforschung und praktischer Beteiligung.* Wiesbaden.

Chatterjee, Tishyarakshit. 2009. Reorienting Environment Policy in India - Towards a Local Area-Based Development and Management Paradigm. *The Journal of Transdisciplinary Environmental Studies* 8(1).

Dienel, Hans-Liudger; Schophaus, Malte. 2002. Bürgerausstellung – ein neues Beteiligungsverfahren für die Stadtplanung. *Forschungsjournal Neue Soziale Bewegungen* 15(2): 90–96.

Dembowski, Hans. 2001. *Taking the State to Court - Public Interest Litigation and the Public Sphere in Metropolitan India.* Oxford.

Jariwala, C.M. 2004. *Environment and Justice.* APH Publishing Corporation, Darya Ganj. Pages 21-45. New Delhi.

Kern, Georg; Reith, Jürgen; Schäfer, Tanja. 2009. Sustainable Transport Planning: Status Report on the Small-Scale Pilot Projects to improve the Traffic Situation in Hyderabad. PTV Report No. 11. Internal Project Report. Karlsruhe.

Kumar, Hari; Sokol, Brian. 2010. Right-to-Know Law Gives India's Poor a Lever. International Herald Tribune. June 28, 2010.

Ministry of Personnel, Public Grievances and Pensions, Department of Administrative Reforms and Public Grievances. 2003. *India Citizen's Charters- A Handbook.* A Publication of the Government of India, New Delhi.

Mohanty, Ranjita; Tandon, Rajesh. 2005. Does Civil Society Matter?: Governance in Contemporary India. Review by Bindu Sharma. *The International Journal of Not-for-Profit Law* 7(2).

Nexus Institute. 2009. Constraints and Opportunities for Participation and Communication. Nexus Deliverable. Internal Project Paper. Berlin.

Poldas, Bhaskar. 2011. Analysing junior college students' awareness of climate change in the emerging megacity of Hyderabad and developing teaching modules to augment their knowledge on the issue. DAAD Report. Hyderabad.

Potsdam Institute for Climate Impact Research (PIK). 2010. Social Representation of Climate Change: A Case Study from Hyderabad (India). Internal Project Paper. Potsdam.

Santhakumar, V. 2009. Will Public Interest Litigations and Citizens' Actions lead to Sustainable Development? An economic analysis with empirical cases from India. *Journal of environment and development economics* Cambridge.

The Hindu. 2010. MMTS Phase II gets the nod. June 6, 2010. http://beta.thehindu.com/news/cities/Hyderabad/article446361.ece?css=print [11-06-10].

ZEENEWS. 2010. SC bifurcates bench to deal with environment work. July 16, 2010. www.zeenews.com/news641514.html [20-07-10].